Strategy
Press

BRAIN
SURGERY
FOR
SUITS

BRAIN SURGERY FOR SUITS

56 THINGS EVERY ACCOUNT PERSON SHOULD KNOW

ROBERT SOLOMON

DRAWINGS BY
RICHARD CLINE

INTRODUCTION BY
MIKE SLOSBERG

STRATEGY PRESS
NEW YORK

Brain Surgery for Suits:
56 things every account person should know
by
Robert Solomon

Published by
Strategy Press
240 Centre Street
New York, NY 10013
USA
strategypress.com

Printed in the United States of America
Library of Congress Cataloging-in-Publication Data
Solomon, Robert J. (Robert Joel)
    Brain surgery for suits : 56 things every
account person should know / by Robert Solomon ;
with drawings by Richard Cline ; and an
introduction by Mike Slosberg. -- 1st ed.
    p. cm.
    LCCN: 99-91500
    ISBN: 0967623499

    1. Customer relations. 2. Customer services.
    3. Success in business. 4. Marketing.
    I. Cline, Richard, ill. II. Slosberg, Mike.
    III. Title.

HF5415.5.S65 2000   658.8'12
                        QBI99-1730

CONTRIBUTORS

HÉLÈNE CÔTÉ

LAUREL CUTLER

HOWARD DRAFT

STEPHEN H. GARDNER

MARK GOLDSTEIN

SHELLEY LANMAN

MICHAEL LOTITO

TOM NELSON

STEVE OLDERMAN

MARTIN PURIS

ROB QUISH

RICHARD P. SHAW

W. DAVID VINING

JEFFREY WILKS

VIVIAN YOUNG

FOR MY MOM

"He who understands everything about his subject cannot write it. I write as much to discover as to explain."

ARTHUR MILLER

INTRODUCTION

I was damn lucky. Over the years I've had the privilege of working with some very exceptional account people. I will never forget them. They helped me succeed. They made me look good and helped me do my very best work. They were equal partners in the quest for solutions, always ready to share the frustration and fun, in equal measure.

Unfortunately, the lame ones — the scared, creatively myopic, politically conniving jerks, the ones we derisively dubbed *conduits of fear* — they stick out in my memory as well. As you might expect, the memories are painful, for they hurt more than they helped. Not just the people they worked with, but the industry as a whole.

A dozen years ago, when I first started working with the author of this book, I recognized pretty quickly that he was one of the exceptional ones. Yes, he was a suit — but as you know, there are cheap suits and there are expensive suits. It was obvious to me that Robert Solomon was a really great suit.

So when he asked me to write the introduction to *Brain Surgery for Suits*, I felt honored.

Then I read the manuscript and I felt excited. Here, finally, was an easy-to-digest codification of the important stuff account people need to know. The ways in which they can guide, inspire, and help creatives create better and more effectively. The subtle techniques of account handling. The right way to prepare for meetings and presentations. How to successfully work with clients—not as a servant but as a partner.

Here in one place—richly packed between two pieces of cardboard—are the secret and precious gems the MBA programs don't know about and can never teach. All the stuff that until now one could only haphazardly pick up from years of hard labor in the business.

So it's up to you: spend the next 10 or 15 years learning this stuff the hard way, or shell out a few bucks and a couple of hours hitchhiking onto what it took Solomon lots of painful years to learn.

Frankly, I would suggest the latter route. Then you can spend your time getting better at what you do, rather than trying to learn what to do.

Mike Slosberg

Co-Founder

Vice Chairman/Chief Creative Officer Emeritus

Digitas

OKAY, SO ACCOUNT WORK ISN'T BRAIN SURGERY.

Brain surgeons undergo years of rigorous training. They work in highly controlled environments. Their word is their command. The work they do is tangible, measurable (the client lives, the client dies), often laudable. They are respected by their staff, their peers, their patients.

Account people get little or no training. They work in chaos. Commands to colleagues, let alone clients, are out of the question. Results are hard to quantify. Forget about respect.

So much of the best account work gets done in the moment—often in private conversations, often in a quick reading of a room—it is nearly impossible to codify what makes a great account person great.

I'll give it a shot anyway.

RS

A WORD ON THE WORD "SUIT."

Several colleagues challenged the book title's reference to account people as "suits." There is a question of political correctness. To some people, the term is always associated with the word "empty." A couple of people said they were offended.

I persisted for three reasons:

1. I wear the label of "suit" proudly and often refer to myself as one. I like its shorthand.

2. "Brain Surgery for Account People" sounds lame.

3. To be an account person requires a tough skin. Account people who are offended by "suit" probably don't like being account people. This book isn't written for them.

RS

CONTENTS

"Rule number one. Move on to rule number two."

20 | PRESCRIPTIONS FOR GREAT ACCOUNT WORK

1 | GREAT WORK WINS BUSINESS; A GREAT RELATIONSHIP KEEPS IT.

In new business pitches, clients often claim they are seeking a *relationship* with an agency, yet select the winner based on which shop presented *the work* they liked best. Conversely, with existing accounts, clients often say it is *the work* that matters, yet fire their agency because of a breakdown in *the relationship*.

Great account people know that when it comes to keeping a client, relationship rules. This explains why the best account people work at the client relationship every day, in ways large and small.

Although everyone in the agency has a role in making the work, it is still the writers who write and the art directors who art direct. The same is true with the client relationship: everyone has a role, from the CEO to the receptionist. But the account people are the ones who field the calls, make the visits, do the lunches, orchestrate the meetings, deliver the follow-up, take the heat, build the trust.

The best work in the world won't keep a client if the relationship goes bad. But it is amazing how the best relationship *can* keep a client, even if the work is far from the best. And that is why every entry in this book is, in some way, about establishing, nurturing, and maintaining the client relationship.

"I found a great way to re-position our brand. Change agencies."

2 | LIVE THE CLIENT'S BRAND.

Don't just buy what your client sells, steep yourself in the brand.

Know the history of the company. Know the people who work there. Observe the culture.

Talk to other people who buy the brand; ask them why.

Know the competitors: their products, their advertising, and, by inference, their marketing strategy.

Read what the press says. Understand what Wall Street thinks. Pay attention to opinion leaders.

Form a point of view on the company and the brand's strengths, weaknesses, opportunities, threats. Always be open to, and seek out, new sources of information and insight.

Think about new ways your client can address a problem or capitalize on an opportunity. Present those thoughts whenever appropriate, and in whatever form and forum are most effective for your client.

———

"I constantly remind account people that they'd never go to someone's home for dinner without bringing flowers or a bottle of wine. For the same reason, they should never go to a client meeting without a gift; in this case, an idea. An idea that says, 'I'm always thinking about ways to build your business or solve tough problems.'"

MARK GOLDSTEIN
Chief Marketing Officer
Fallon McElligott

3 | TAKE ON THE COLORATION OF YOUR CLIENTS; DO NOT COMPROMISE YOUR CHARACTER.

The best account people are chameleons. They can talk about most anything, and are interested in everything.

They are voracious consumers of popular culture, and are at least on passing terms with higher-brow pursuits. They have fun with beer-guzzling, football-loving clients. They have fun with champagne-quaffing, theatergoing clients. It's not acting. It's real.

Great account people are superb listeners. They take a sincere interest in their clients — professionally and personally — while being respectful of their privacy. They never force the relationship; they nurture it patiently, over time.

The best account people are flexible and open-minded, able to handle the unexpected with grace. They are this way because they know exactly where to draw the line they won't cross, not this time, not ever. They never violate their own integrity, honesty, or sense of fairness.

4 NO MATTER HOW SOCIAL IT BECOMES, NEVER FORGET IT IS BUSINESS.

Do not mistake your relationship for personal friendship. That person sitting across from you is *always* your client.

Watch what you drink, watch how you behave, and above all, watch what you say. No tales out of school, no alcohol talking.

5 | YOU CANNOT LEAD AN ACCOUNT FROM YOUR DESK.

Account work is field work. Visit your clients regularly, no matter if they are on the next street or in the next time zone. Phone calls and e-mails don't replace face time.

Do not wait for trouble to get off your butt. The time to spend time with clients — to build your relationship with them — is when things are going well. Most clients have little patience for account people who only show up when something goes wrong. And if that is the only time you see your client, you won't have forged the relationship you need in order to fix the problem you are there to address.

With client visits, the question is, "How often is enough?" There is no one right answer; it depends on the client. But it is almost impossible to spend too much time with clients. So, if you lack a specific reason to see your clients, create one. And if you can't figure out how to do that, find another line of work.

6

THERE IS NO SUCH THING AS TOO MUCH COMMUNICATION.

Walk the halls, pick up the phone, always be available to clients and colleagues.

Follow up every meeting, every call, every decision. Never assume there is closure; secure closure. Make sure everyone understands and agrees with the decisions made and the next steps to be taken.

"Call them, but, before that, let me call them. I should talk to them so that they know that I've talked to you, so that when you've called them, they will have talked to me."

7 | MAKE NO COMMITMENT WITHOUT CONSULTATION.

When a client makes a request, let alone a demand, your first, and understandable, instinct is to say "yes." The more senior the client, the more urgent the need, the more strident the tone, the more you want to comply on the spot.

Don't.

Even with seemingly simple requests, a unilateral "yes" is *not* the right answer. It does a terrible disservice to everyone — your colleagues, yourself, and most of all, your client.

A commitment without consultation ignores the collaborative nature of making advertising. It pays no respect to the people you work with. Besides, you may not be able to deliver on your commitment.

You may be a big fish in the agency food chain. You may have the power to say "yes." But you and your client will soon feel the consequences of the unchecked exercise of that power. It will undermine teamwork, it will erode morale, it will destroy your credibility.

The fact is, the more senior you are, the easier it is to explain to your client that you want to check with others first before saying "yes."

But that doesn't mean you say "no" either. (See prescription #8.)

The exact answer you give will of course depend on the circumstances. But it generally should go something like this: "I *think* it will be fine, but give me a minute to check, then get back to you."

Get to your colleagues, gain consensus, then get back to your client, without delay. Your client needs an answer, quickly, that all of you can live with.

8 | THERE IS NO "NO" IN YOUR CLIENT VOCABULARY.

Your job is to build bridges, not barriers. "No" is a barrier-builder.

So, even when a client makes a seemingly unreasonable request — about a deadline, about a budget, about a change in the work — "no" is not the answer. "No" helps no one — not the agency, not your colleagues, and of course, not the clients.

What is the right answer?

First, remember prescription #7: no commitment without consultation. But even after you've spoken with your colleagues, you still may not be able to give your clients exactly what they want.

When an unqualified "yes" isn't possible, offer a qualified one: "Here's what we can do; it's not a perfect solution, but does it address your need?"

Discuss, negotiate, collaborate, solve the problem together. Even difficult clients will usually accept a reasonable solution, especially when you've made every effort to give them what they want.

9

BEFORE YOU TELL CLIENTS OR COLLEAGUES WHAT YOU THINK, TELL THEM WHAT YOU KNOW.

Everyone has an opinion. Before you render yours, deliver the facts needed for informed decision making.

10 BEFORE YOU GIVE CLIENTS WHAT THEY NEED, MAKE SURE YOU GIVE THEM WHAT THEY WANT.

Resist the temptation to save clients from themselves. If they make a decision, respect it. If you think the decision is wrongheaded, offer an alternative approach.

Given a choice, clients will usually do the right thing. But don't presume to make the decision for them by giving them only what you think they need.

11 FIGHT **ABOUT** THE WORK WITH COLLEAGUES, FIGHT **FOR** IT WITH CLIENTS.

You owe your colleagues insightful, expert, candid, and sensitive assessment of their work. You should base this assessment on the strategy driving the work, your knowledge of the competitive market, your grasp of the consumer's needs and interests, and your understanding of client expectations and culture.

You and your colleagues won't always agree. You will argue; happily or not, this often is part of arriving at the right solution.

It's fine to fight about the work in private, but once you've agreed on what to present to the client, get on the bus. When you are in front of the client, never throw the work, or your colleagues, under the bus.

"Here's what I expect (or to be more precise, pray for) from account people.

"I want them to love the creative work. I want them to care about it, be knowledgeable about it. Gush when it's great. Blow the whistle when it's bad. I want passion. Otherwise, the ad, or mail piece, or website is just another deliverable, judged only by whether it's on time and on budget.

"Creative people will do just about anything for an account person who says, 'I love that.'

"As for account people, imagine how much more satisfying their jobs can be if they really get involved with the work instead of just delivering it from the agency to the client."

STEVE OLDERMAN
Executive Vice President
Executive Creative Director
Digitas

12 | ALWAYS THINK ENDGAME.

Do not give in to the temptation to win the argument; think instead of what's going to get the result the client needs.

13 | NO SURPRISES ABOUT MONEY OR TIME.

Advise clients up front about the cost and timing implications of their decisions. This allows them to make fully informed choices. And it allows you to avoid any after-the-fact surprises that result in painful consequences, ranging from a loss of money to a loss of trust.

14 | DEAL WITH TROUBLE HEAD-ON.

Advertising is people-intensive. Given the number of hands that touch even the simplest assignment, it is astonishing how much work gets produced error-free.

Still, things get derailed; on occasion, there is a full-scale train wreck. A deadline gets blown. There is a mistake in the ad. The wrong spot gets shipped.

When something goes awry, get to your client with a full explanation of what happened and why. Whenever possible, be prepared to outline one or more ways to address the problem. Move quickly; *you* want to deliver the bad news to the client. You don't want them to hear it from another source.

If the agency is on the hook for serious money, get senior management involved immediately; work out what you are prepared to do financially before you call the client. Volunteer the financial solution before the client asks for it.

Above all, never, ever lie to your client. Sure, you might get away with it this time. But at some point, you won't. And once you're caught in a lie, your single greatest asset — your credibility — will be gone forever.

———

"The best account people have such a profound sense of responsibility that they literally find a way to blame themselves for anything that goes wrong."

STEPHEN H. GARDNER
President
The Gardner-Nelson Project

15 | BE BRIEF, BE BRIGHT, BE GONE.

Come to the table prepared. Know what you want to say; know what you want the outcome of the meeting, the call, or the presentation to be. Make your points clearly, quickly, concisely. Don't waste your clients' or colleagues' time.

Above all, know when to close your briefcase. Once you have buy-in, do not run on at the mouth; run out the door instead.

16 | BETTER TO HAVE IT AND NOT NEED IT, THAN NEED IT AND NOT HAVE IT.

There is no such thing as being over-prepared for a client meeting or presentation. Take the time to create and compile all the materials you might possibly need to make the meeting a success. Anticipate the questions that will arise in the discussion; be ready to respond.

———

"Whenever I am asked to interview account service candidates and determine if they will be good creative partners, I always look for one big indicator.

"A book of the work they helped to shape.

"It immediately speaks to the pride, empathy and sense of shared ownership they bring. It also says a lot about their ability to nurture, support and sell-in good work. I'm always amazed at how few of these candidates even bother to put a book together, but when I see one, I make sure they don't get away."

HÉLÈNE CÔTÉ
Executive Vice President
Executive Creative Director, NY
Rapp Collins Worldwide

17 | ONCE A CLIENT, ALWAYS A CLIENT.

Not all clients welcome this, but if they do, stay in touch even after they become former clients.

When they move on, drop them a note of best wishes. Keep them on your personal mailing list. Send an e-mail once in a while; clip an article for them.

If your relationship warrants it, call them periodically. Even better, if you can get together for a meal or a drink, do it.

Above all, never burn a bridge. You never know where a former client will end up. That person might be a new business prospect, or a client again, or your colleague, or even your boss.

18

FORGET WHAT STANLEY MOTSS* SAID: "I WANT THE CREDIT."

Credit is for creative directors.

* Played by Dustin Hoffman in *Wag the Dog*.

19 | IF THINGS GO WRONG, TAKE THE BLAME.

You provide air cover for everyone in the agency. If something goes wrong in media, in creative, in production, it happened on your watch. You are responsible. You are the one who takes the heat from the client.

It's not fun. It's your job. Get used to it.

"We speak with one voice here. This way, when things go well, I can accept all applause. When things go wrong, I can tell everyone else they're wrong."

20 | JUDGEMENT OVERRIDES ANY RULE.

All great account people have unfailingly good judgement. They are quick on their feet. They know exactly what to say or do, and how, in the moment. They can defuse a bomb or perform triage in the most trying circumstance.

No rule can accommodate every situation; no list of rules is exhaustive. In the end, your judgement must rule.

———

"The job of account executive is the most difficult in the agency business. It's an intellectual high-wire act.

"The two fatal mistakes an account person can make are to become either the client's 'man' at the agency — or the agency's 'man' at the client.

"Both fail.

"A good account person gives us objectivity, commitment, insight and — above all — truth."

MARTIN PURIS
Former Chairman, CEO
Chief Creative Officer
Ammirati Puris Lintas

20 PRESCRIPTIONS FOR GREAT ACCOUNT WORK

1. Great work wins business; a great relationship keeps it.
2. Live the client's brand.
3. Take on the coloration of your clients; do not compromise your character.
4. No matter how social it becomes, never forget it is business.
5. You cannot lead an account from your desk.
6. There is no such thing as too much communication.
7. Make no commitment without consultation.
8. There is no "no" in your client vocabulary.
9. Before you tell clients or colleagues what you *think*, tell them what you *know*.
10. Before you give clients what they *need*, make sure you give them what they *want*.

11. Fight *about* the work with colleagues, fight *for* it with clients.
12. Always think endgame.
13. No surprises about money or time.
14. Deal with trouble head-on.
15. Be brief, be bright, be gone.
16. Better to have it and not need it, than need it and not have it.
17. Once a client, always a client.
18. Forget what Stanley Motss said: "I want the credit."
19. If things go wrong, take the blame.
20. Judgement overrides any rule.

4 STEPS TO TAKE AT THE START OF ANY ASSIGNMENT

21

ALWAYS MANAGE CLIENT EXPECTATIONS FROM THE OUTSET.

Make sure your clients understand how you and your colleagues will be approaching the assignment. What the steps are. What the agency will deliver at each step. When they will see work, and in what form. Who will present it. If you need the clients to be at the agency, let them know, so they can plan accordingly.

Listen carefully for any client concerns, even when they are not stated overtly. Especially when they are not stated overtly. Ask questions. Probe. Draw the clients out.

If the clients are uncomfortable about any step you're planning to take to execute the assignment, work out a solution that will make them comfortable. Follow up to make sure there are no lingering issues.

22 | DEFINE SUCCESS.

Too often, agency people will begin work on an assignment without asking the client, "What do you want to achieve with this advertising?"

Begin every client relationship, and every client advertising effort, with a clear understanding of the client's goals. The business goals. The sales goals. The communication goals. The response they are seeking from *inside* the company, both management *and* staff. Their *personal* goals.

Never lose sight of those goals in the process of making the advertising. They are a yardstick by which to determine if the work — and the relationship — are on course.

———

"Sometimes the biggest challenge facing an account person is actually making a bold decision — and sticking to it. Sometimes you just have to step out on a limb."

HOWARD DRAFT
Chairman and CEO
Draft Worldwide

23 | START WITH AN AGREED-ON STRATEGY, BUDGET, AND SCHEDULE.

In a world where every client wants it yesterday and every assignment is a rush job, it is tempting to take short-cuts. Forget the budget. Forget the schedule. And who needs a strategy? We'll just wing it.

But there is a saying, "There is always time to do it over." If you subvert the very processes that help you and your colleagues get it right the *first* time, you surely will find yourselves working to get it right the *second* time.

As a result, no time will have been saved; chances are the assignment will take longer than if, at the outset, you ran the numbers, wrote the budget, and agreed on a strategy.

Strive to keep these steps in the process, even when it

appears it would be faster to forego them. Otherwise, you risk chaos. Not to speak of bad advertising.

24

ASK YOURSELF, "WHAT DO MY COLLEAGUES NEED TO CREATE GREAT ADVERTISING?" THEN DELIVER IT.

Be a resource to your colleagues. Do give them key facts and critical insights. Do share what the client is saying to you. Do show them the work the competitors are running. Do not drown them in data.

Be available to help, in any and every way you can. If the creative team is working late, stay late with them, or at least be available by phone and e-mail. If they're working the weekend, work the weekend with them. If you want to deliver great work to your client, you must be a partner in the process.

———

"Be unstoppably curious. Feel a deep sense of responsibility for the creative product. Know intelligence and passion build trust and gain a following."

ROB QUISH

President, New York

Lowe Lintas & Partners

4 STEPS TO TAKE AT THE START OF ANY ASSIGNMENT

21. Always manage client expectations from the outset.
22. Define success.
23. Start with an agreed-on strategy, budget, and schedule.
24. Ask yourself, "What do my colleagues need to create great advertising?" Then deliver it.

5 | PROCEDURES FOR A STRATEGY BRIEF

25 | PROVIDE THE CLIENT'S PERSPECTIVE.

No one knows the client — its products, its people, its culture — better than you. You've walked the halls of company headquarters every week. You've been out in the field with the salespeople, talking with customers and prospects. You've lost count of the number of breakfasts, lunches, and dinners you've had with client people, at all levels and in many different departments.

You watch and read every competitive ad; you follow the trade and business press. You listen to Wall Street. You regularly visit the client's website. You are a customer.

In short, you live the brand. It gives you a perspective that helps sharpen and define the strategy. It can help uncover the overlooked fact that can drive an insight that can lead to an idea that can result in killer advertising.

Do that, and you'll be a hero to your colleagues.

———

"A great account person should be able to help clients innovate and to deliver ingenious solutions to critical marketing issues."

RICHARD P. SHAW
Vice President
Global Marketing Communications
Seagram Spirits And Wine Group

26 | INVOLVE THE
CREATIVE TEAM.

There are four reasons to do this: 1) to help the creative people immerse themselves in the assignment; 2) to uncover issues, concerns, or gaps in knowledge early on in the process; 3) to uncover insights or connections that otherwise might be missed; and 4) to ensure that the strategy brief actually assists in the creation of effective advertising.

"Let's have a charming dialogue, and then you can do what I want."

27 GET THE CLIENT'S INPUT AND APPROVAL.

The development of the strategy brief is part of the creative process, not separate from it. You want the client's input while you and your colleagues are collaborating on the brief. You want the client's signed approval on the brief once it's done.

The brief will serve as a means to evaluate the creative that will emerge from it. If your client does not participate in its formulation, or if your client does not sign off on the final version that will drive the work, trouble is sure to follow. You've seen clients use the creative work to rethink the strategy.

That's a backward way of working. It takes extra time, it wastes money, and it doesn't help make great work.

28 | TAKE THE WORD "BRIEF" SERIOUSLY.

There's a saying, "I didn't have time to write you a short letter, so I wrote you a long one." Brevity is hard work. The key to achieving it lies not in writing, but in rewriting, rewriting, rewriting.

With a creative brief, the goal is no wasted words. There should be a distillation of key facts. A precise objective. A clear understanding of the problem the advertising has to solve. An outline of tone, manner, mandatories. A couple of pages, max.

Why is brevity important? A brief that isn't brief is no help to anyone. The reader can't distinguish the important points from the underbrush of detail in which they are hidden. The client won't embrace it, the creative team won't follow it, and the work will suffer because of it.

29 | KNOW WHEN TO LOOK IT UP; KNOW WHEN TO MAKE IT UP.

One clear insight is worth a thousand data points. There's a time to put the research away, and go with your instinct. Don't let information interfere with understanding; combine what you know with what you feel in order to push for new ideas and better solutions.

———

"Here's my take on what differentiates the great account person from the good...

A gift for recognizing potential.

The potential in a client's product.

The potential in a new strategic direction or a nascent creative idea.

And an almost psychic ability to anticipate and prevent potential disaster."

VIVIAN YOUNG
Strategic Counselor
Lowe Lintas & Partners

5 PROCEDURES FOR A STRATEGY BRIEF

25. Provide the client's perspective.
26. Involve the creative team.
27. Get the client's input and approval.
28. Take the word "brief" seriously.
29. Know when to look it up; know when to make it up.

7 | REMINDERS ABOUT MAKING GREAT CREATIVE

30

ALWAYS ASK YOURSELF, "DOES THIS ADVERTISING PASS THE 'SO WHAT' TEST?"

The airwaves are filled with ads that, at best, put the viewer to sleep. At worst, they debase the client's brand, rather than build it.

It is not enough for the work to be on strategy; it has to engage consumers, influence how they think and what they feel, and cause them to act.

Whenever you're reviewing work with your creative colleagues, first ask yourself if it is on strategy. Then ask yourself if it makes you think, "So what."

If the work doesn't pass the "so what" test, it will never pass the test of the marketplace. So don't present it to the client. Instead, keep working.

"Not now, Ms. Myers, we're reverberating."

31

DON'T FALL IN LOVE WITH GOOD WORK.

Good work is on strategy. It's smart, it respects the viewer, it's well crafted. You can produce it on time, and on budget. Your client will green-light it. It makes you comfortable.

Good work is the enemy of great work. If you are satisfied with work that is merely good, you will never deliver great work for your clients.

Great work, like good work, is on strategy. But it's not just smart, it's brilliant. It doesn't just respect the viewer, it connects with the viewer.

Great work might make you uncomfortable. It might be something startlingly new. It might take risks. You might not be able to produce it on time or within budget. And your client might not readily say "yes" to it.

But if the work is truly great, and right for your client, your job is to support it, and to help your client buy it.

———

"The best account people know the clients' idiosyncrasies but don't take them too seriously. Nor do they take themselves too seriously. They do, of course, take the creative very seriously."

SHELLEY LANMAN
Executive Vice President
Executive Creative Director
Draft Worldwide

32 | DON'T FALL FOR BAD WORK.

What passes for great work these days is often little more than a clever execution or an unusual production technique.

Work like this can be insidious; it masquerades as great advertising, but instead sacrifices the client's advertising objective on the altar of creative self-indulgence.

Great account people have the judgement and discipline needed to see such work for what it is; they are not blinded by its superficial appeal. They rely on the courage of their convictions and their credibility with colleagues to root it out.

Unmasking work like this can be a difficult, dangerous job, requiring patience, perseverance, diplomacy, and large amounts of political capital. But it is even more dan-

gerous to ignore work like this, and allow it to be produced. It can cost account people their credibility. It can
cost the agency an account.

33 | CHOICE IS GOOD.

There is always more than one way to execute a strategy. If you offer your clients just one execution, you are putting them in a "take it or leave it" situation, which is no choice at all.

Bring your clients more than one option. Three is an ideal number. More than five is confusing, and implies you are surrounding the strategic challenge, rather than solving it.

Agree on an agency recommendation before you meet with your client. But make sure you would be proud to produce anything you show. There should be no straw men among the options.

34 | DO NOT "SELL."

Selling is about applying pressure on a buyer to do what you want — what is best for you, your colleagues, your agency. There is a temptation to "sell," to prove your worth to your creative colleagues.

Do not give in to this mindset. It won't help you, your colleagues, or your agency deliver what your client wants and needs.

You are not a salesperson; you are a partner to your agency colleagues, and to your client. Your role is to facilitate the creation of great work, and to help your client make the right decisions about the work.

———

"Too often, a creative-driven agency will try to force their own ideas on a client, rather than working in a spirit of collaboration. It takes a very strong account person to maintain the client's interest, and not take the easy way out by simply selling the work."

W. DAVID VINING
Director, Customer Marketing
E*Trade

35 | BRING YOUR CLIENTS INTO THE PROCESS EARLY.

Advertising isn't just about collaboration within the walls of the agency, it's a collaboration with the client.

Having the client's perspective early helps avoid false starts. No matter how well versed you are in the brand, your client brings a critical point of view to the process.

Early involvement also gives the client a sense of ownership of the work. This, in turn, helps the client partner with the agency in presenting the work to others who must approve and embrace it.

"<u>Okay</u>. Phase one. We think of ideas to throw at the client. Phase two, we pitch the ideas. Phase three, we listen to what they want and throw everything <u>we</u> think out the window."

36 | RESPECT WHAT IT TAKES TO DO GREAT CREATIVE.

What it takes is enormous emotional commitment.

When writers or art directors show their work, they are sharing a piece of themselves. They have sweated that idea to life. If you don't respect that, you have no hope of helping make the work better.

But, while it takes emotional commitment to make creative work, it takes emotional detachment to make it better. Creative people don't always have this. You do. *How* you provide the input that comes from that detachment is key.

If you're looking at a range of ideas, and one is a killer, one has potential, and one needs to be killed, start with the killer. Make sure you acknowledge what you love about it and why.

Then, with the work that has potential, start with

what's right about it. Praise that. Then suggest how it can be made better.

End with the idea that deserves an early death. But, even with the most marginal of ideas, there is inevitably *something* to like about it. Find that one thing, and acknowledge it, before suggesting the idea be abandoned.

Keep your personal preferences out of the discussion. You are not there to render judgement on whether or not periwinkle is the right color. However, if you know the client hates periwinkle, or if periwinkle is the competitor's brand color, by all means speak up.

You are there to ensure the work is on strategy. To bring a client perspective to the discussion. To measure the work against what is going on in the category. To help determine if the work passes the "so what" test. To check that no mandatory has been missed.

And, above all, to push for great, if what you're seeing is merely good.

———

"In my experience, account people spend too much time talking about 'partnership' and not enough time practicing it. For your creative team, a detailed 16-point memo after the big presentation is no substitute for a lukewarm quart of Szechuan noodles the night before."

TOM NELSON

Creative Director

The Gardner-Nelson Project

7 REMINDERS ABOUT MAKING GREAT CREATIVE

30. Always ask yourself, "Does this advertising pass the 'so what' test?"
31. Don't fall in love with good work.
32. Don't fall for bad work.
33. Choice is good.
34. Do not "sell."
35. Bring your clients into the process early.
36. Respect what it takes to do great creative.

8 | THOUGHTS ON CLIENT PRESENTATIONS

37

CLIENT PRESENTATIONS
ARE AS IMPORTANT
AS NEW BUSINESS
PRESENTATIONS.

Agencies treat new business presentations with the intensity and urgency of opening night at the theater.

Everyone understands what's at stake. There is careful consideration given to casting the presenters. There is heavy investment in staging and props. Every word of the script is thought through. The pitch team rehearses. Then it rehearses some more.

With client business, people are so busy making the work, they often neglect the presenting part. But client presentations are as important as new business presentations. The stakes are just as high, if not higher. The only thing worse than losing a new business pitch is losing a client. If you don't pay attention to client presentations, if you take them for granted, that is the risk.

Client presentations, like new business presentations, are about theater. Bad theater often leads to a bad ending, with the client leaving unhappy and the agency left to regroup. Good theater usually leads to a good ending, with the client satisfied and the work approved.

Good theater is no accident. It requires proper casting, with an eye to who can best deliver the material. It requires thoughtful preparation, with particular attention paid to anticipating client concerns and how best to address them. Above all, it requires sufficient time to rehearse, to ensure everyone understands their roles and how to play them.

Agencies forget this. Great account people remind them, and find a way to ensure that the agency is ready on presentation day, no matter how pressed for time everyone is.

————

"Alignment is the indispensable contribution of the account guy. Getting all the levels of the client marching in the same direction with the agency creative and planning forces to help the prime prospect consumer realize his aspiration. The overarching goal is helping our customer position himself."

LAUREL CUTLER
Member, Board of Directors
Fallon McElligott

38 | NO UNDERSTUDIES ON PRESENTATION DAY.

It's important to give junior people a chance to present. How else will they learn? But those learning opportunities need to be confined to *internal* agency presentations, until that star of the future has earned a role in the present, and is proven ready to perform in front of the client.

Until that time, presenting to the client should be left to those most effective at it, and that usually means the more senior people in the shop (any senior person who is a weak presenter needs to address that weakness). There is too much riding on the presentation to do otherwise.

You are not only presenting work, you are representing the agency. And every presentation offers an opportunity to validate the client's confidence in the agency, or conversely, to undermine it.

So, no understudies on presentation day. Let the veterans, the stars, perform. That is what the client has a right to expect. That is what the client is paying for. And that is what will keep the business right where it is.

39 | NO SCENERY CHEWERS;
NO DEAD BODIES.

Advertising is about collaboration. So is the presentation of advertising. It is not a one-person show; it is an ensemble performance. There should be no scenery chewers who have all the lines, and who completely dominate the stage.

By the same token, there should be no dead bodies. Everyone present from the agency should have a role. You don't want clients asking themselves, "Why is that person here? What value is that person adding? Why am I paying for that person?"

40 | BE PREPARED TO THROW AWAY THE SCRIPT.

Just because you've prepared doesn't mean you'll get to present exactly the way you intended. Clients have their own agendas, and you need to be willing to bend yours to theirs. If they want the presentation to go in a different way than you planned it, you should be ready to adjust.

What's the point of insisting on your agenda, only to have your words land on a tuned-out audience? Be flexible, fast on your feet, and ready to ad-lib.

41 | THE MORE INFORMAL YOU WANT TO BE, THE MORE REHEARSED YOU NEED TO BE.

If you're presenting with PowerPoint (or some other presentation software), if you're relying on charts or boards, if you're reading from notes, presenting is relatively easy. You have a safety net under you.

However, if you're *talking* to your audience, rather than *presenting* to it — without computer slides, without notes — you are working without a net. It's harder and riskier. But it's often more effective.

These "casual" presenters — those who can talk their presentation with an appearance of ease — are the ones who inevitably are the best rehearsed. It is a rare person who can wing it and do well.

The more you want to work without a net, the better

prepared you need to be. Take the time needed to script yourself, to learn your lines, to hone your delivery.

"Don't tell me anything about the presentation. It's better I know nothing."

42 | KNOW YOUR OPENING COLD.

If you're going to screw up, it will happen in your opening. That's why you want to know your opening the way you know the first words of the "Gettysburg Address."

After you nail the opening, you'll relax. And when you relax, the rest of your presentation will flow. You will enjoy yourself. It will show, and the presentation will be a success.

43 | SUPPORT WHAT YOU SAY.

Check your presentation for the claims it makes. If you can't support an assertion, find another way to state it, or don't make it. Instead of building your argument, an unsupported claim will undermine it. It can leave you open to challenge, which can derail your presentation, and the work.

44 | LISTENING IS MORE IMPORTANT THAN TALKING.

If, at the end of your presentation, you and your colleagues have done all the talking, you will know that you have failed.

The point isn't to deliver your lines exactly as rehearsed. The point is to engage your client, as early and as often as possible, in a discussion that leads to agreement. If you get to dialogue, you've taken the first step toward accomplishing this.

———

"A great account person is one who can help in the creation of great advertising through a combination of strategic insight and proven creative taste. The reason a great account person is so rare Is that these two talents arise out of different sides of the brain. In effect, great account people must be equally adept at left brain and right brain talents.

"Above all, they must be able to build and sustain meaningful relationships with all types of people — from the most artsy creative person to the most analytical media person — from the most type A client to the most laid back producer. This means being a great salesman without the sleazy part of selling. And it means having a thick skin. Account people take the brunt of most problem venting."

MICHAEL LOTITO
President/COO
Initiative Media North America

8 THOUGHTS ON CLIENT PRESENTATIONS

37. Client presentations are as important as new business presentations.
38. No understudies on presentation day.
39. No scenery chewers; no dead bodies.
40. Be prepared to throw away the script.
41. The more informal you want to be, the more rehearsed you need to be.
42. Know your opening cold.
43. Support what you say.
44. Listening is more important than talking.

4 | ELEMENTS OF BETTER MEETING MANAGEMENT

45 | START ON TIME,
END ON TIME.

With client meetings, this is doable. Most agency people respect the need to be punctual with the client. The challenge is to get the client to be on time. If they come from a company culture that expects punctuality, you'll have no problem. If they don't, you will, and you'll have to address the issue.

One option is to *gently* remind clients they are paying for all those people cooling their heels in the conference room.

With internal meetings, it is easy to talk punctuality, hard to be punctual. Your time is not your own; you are on call to your client. Even if you are disciplined about being on time, often your colleagues are not.

The trick with internal meetings is to treat them with

the respect you accord client meetings. If *you* show up on time, begin on time, and end as promised, people will begin to follow the example you set. You'll never get 100 percent compliance, but you need to strive for it.

46 | HAVE AN AGENDA, STICK TO IT.

Every meeting requires an agenda. The process of creating one in advance helps you determine what needs to be accomplished. It also gives you a way to solicit input. This is particularly important when preparing for client meetings. You want your client's input before you get in the conference room.

At the meeting itself, the agenda provides focus and helps everyone be efficient and productive. And coming to the meeting prepared demonstrates your respect for other people's time. But...

Remember an agenda is not written in stone. Remain flexible, especially with your client. Start the meeting by asking if everyone is comfortable with what is planned. Be open to additions, deletions, an adjustment in the order of things, or any other sensible change.

47

LEAD THE MEETING,
DON'T DOMINATE IT.

With the meeting objectives clearly in mind, your job is to guide the discussion. You must keep everyone on track. Your goal is to accomplish what needs to be accomplished, while leaving room for the unexpected. You must allow all voices to be heard, and actively seek participation from those reluctant to come forward.

In-person meetings are easy to run compared with teleconferences. But, especially with out-of-town clients, teleconferences are an unfortunate reality.

On the speakerphone you don't have the advantage of face-to-face contact, or the cues of body language. Voice inflections become muddy. You must be ever-vigilant to hear all views. You must listen for the subtext of every client comment. Seek clarification during the teleconference. If you judge it more appropriate to have a private discussion, follow up later with your client, one-to-one, over the phone.

End every meeting with an oral recap of decisions reached and next steps to be taken (that means taking good notes during the discussion). If it's a client meeting, make certain your client is satisfied with the outcome.

"I listen to everyone, but in the end, I am most deeply influenced by me."

48 | ALWAYS FOLLOW UP.

The oral recap at meeting's end is not sufficient. Immediately after the meeting concludes, follow up with an e-mail conference report. It is *not* necessary to revisit the discussion. Simply bullet the decisions reached and next steps required.

You should do this for all meetings, but it is crucial for client meetings, because it provides an audit trail. Should a dispute arise later in the process, the documentation will quickly show who agreed to what, and when.

———

"Three rules of great account management:

1. Communicate better than anyone else.

2. Strive for efficiency in creating solutions to the problems you face, but rigorously avoid the expedient options.

3. View knowledge accumulation as both a mechanism for differentiating yourself and a process that never ceases."

JEFFREY WILKS
Executive Vice President
Senior Account Director
BBDO New York

4 ELEMENTS OF BETTER MEETING MANAGEMENT

45. Start on time, end on time.
46. Have an agenda, stick to it.
47. Lead the meeting, don't dominate it.
48. Always follow up.

2 | BOOKS TO READ AND REREAD

49 | <u>THE ELEMENTS OF STYLE</u>.

Great account people write with uncommon clarity and brevity. Their correspondence, presentations, briefs, and memos are precise, perfectly organized, and fast reading. Their prose is a pleasure to read, never a chore.

William Strunk and E.B. White's *The Elements of Style* is an elegant guide to better writing. Take it with you on your next business trip; spend an hour with it. Then, the next time you sit down to write, you'll write better.

50 |

If *The Elements of Style* is the best book on writing, surely William Zinsser's *On Writing Well* is a close second. The chapters on "Simplicity," "Clutter," and "Style" are particularly helpful.

As Zinsser states, "Writing is hard work. A clear sentence is no accident. Very few sentences come out right the first time, or even the third time. Remember this in moments of despair. If you find writing is hard, it is because it *is* hard."

2 BOOKS TO READ AND REREAD

49. *The Elements of Style*, by William Strunk and E.B. White, fourth edition published in 1999 by Allyn & Bacon.
50. *On Writing Well*, by William Zinsser, sixth edition published in 1998 by HarperCollins.

1 | SUGGESTION ON BEING A CONCIERGE TO YOUR CLIENTS

51 | BE ONE.

You want your clients to look forward to coming to the agency. That means making every visit a superb experience, using each one to build the relationship.

If your clients are coming from out of town, meet their plane, or have a reliable car service, one you know well, meet and bring them to the city (in a sedan, not a stretch).

Offer to make the hotel reservations. If the clients prefer to do this on their own, do not press. Either way, have an amenity in their rooms on their arrival (a bottle of mineral water, fresh fruit, or flowers), with a welcome note from you and the agency. If you can arrange for complimentary room upgrades without intruding on your clients' privacy, do so. Arrange for transportation to and from the hotel — to the agency, back to the airport — throughout your clients' stay.

If your clients are willing to have dinner with you before or after the meeting, choose a restaurant that 1) you know well; 2) will make your clients feel both comfortable and special; 3) is quiet enough to conduct a conversation. Take into account your client's food preferences and special needs.

Cast the dinner with care. Who do the clients know and like? Who do they need to meet, or get to know better? Who is good at these events?

Generally follow the rule of having no more than two agency people for every client person in attendance. More than two agency people per client makes the dinner look like a boondoggle. That is not the impression you want to make on your clients, your colleagues, or your management.

A small group is better for business; a large group is better for fun. "Fun" is a legitimate client-dinner objective.

If it's a large group, have place cards, so you can orchestrate a seating arrangement that meets your business needs. Have a special menu prepared in advance; it simplifies the evening; it removes prices from view. Talk to the restaurant manager ahead of time about where your group will be placed in the dining room; if it's preferable to have a private room, arrange for one.

Run any dinner, large or small, as you would a meeting. Start on time. Oversee the conversation but do not dominate it.

Keep it lively: conduct a wine tasting (or a beer tasting), share some appetizers, have the chef talk about the menu, make some toasts, whatever is appropriate for the event. Handle the bill in advance, so you don't have to do this in front of your clients.

Always watch what you drink. Keep an eye out for cues from your clients, spoken or nonverbal. End the evening early if you are meeting the following morning (or if the clients are leaving early). Follow up with a note of thanks to the clients that tells them how much you and your colleagues enjoyed spending time with them away from work.

1 SUGGESTION ON BEING A CONCIERGE TO YOUR CLIENTS

51. Be one.

4 | POINTS OF VIEW
ON PERSONAL STYLE

52 | MAKE AN INVESTMENT IN YOURSELF.

You are the agency's lead representative to your client. Grooming counts. It can affect how others see you, and how they judge your work. It can affect how you feel about yourself.

So do what it takes to get the styling details right, from a decent haircut to decent shoes, and everything in between. It's more about investing time and attention than dollars and cents.

53

BUY FEWER, BETTER PIECES OF TAILORED CLOTHING.

The great thing about the "casualization" of corporate America is you no longer need a closet full of business suits (a lower dry-cleaning bill is a plus too). A couple of suits — three or four at most — will do for most account people. Make them basic in color and pattern. Use accessories to create variety, to achieve the right look for the occasion, and to stave off boredom.

Because you need fewer suits in your wardrobe, you should be able to invest in some upgrading.

This doesn't have to be about designer labels. In fact, it's better to find a good tailor and have a couple of suits made for you. Doing so can cost less than many of the top labels, the clothes will fit better, and you'll have an opportunity to express your personal style in the tailoring details.

54 | ASK FOR STYLE HELP IF YOU NEED IT.

The next time you leave home for work, stop first to take a long, clear look in the mirror. If you don't have what it takes to style yourself, admit it and find some help.

In most agencies there are people with terrific style sense. Choose the person whose look you most admire and feel comfortable with. Drag her or him shopping with you.

Let your newly recruited style adviser make you smarter about what works on you. But make sure you are comfortable with your adviser's recommendations. Do not allow yourself to be talked into anything that does not feel right.

5 5 | THINK UNIFORM.

For many people casual attire is tougher than business wear. The rules, such as they are, are less clear. It takes more confidence, and fashion sense, to "do casual" well.

One way to address this is to figure out a casual "uniform" that works for you, and simply wear that look most, if not all, the time. If you need variety, change the accessories.

Shopping is easier, packing for the road is a cinch, and there's no "what do I wear today" anxiety in the morning (you have more important things to worry about).

"Do you have anything slightly more pretentious?"

4 POINTS OF VIEW
ON PERSONAL STYLE

52. Make an investment in yourself.

53. Buy fewer, better pieces of tailored clothing.

54. Ask for style help if you need it.

55. Think uniform.

1 | MORE THING TO REMEMBER

56 | REMEMBER TO SAY THANK YOU.

Account service people cannot say "thank you" too often. I'm about to follow this rule; thank you for bearing with me.

I've been fortunate to work with many terrific people. I've learned something from every relationship, not just the ones my weak memory has allowed me to acknowledge below.

In the early 1980s, when Dan Paisley was a principal at the agency Paisley, Romorini & Canby, and I was his client, he inspired me to think about going agency side.

Michael Bronner gave me my first agency job, back in the days when Bronner Slosberg was known as Eastern Exclusives. While there, my first account service teachers were Kristen Wainwright and Harry Barrett. John

Fletcher, Brinton Young, and T. Campbell Edlund provided early lessons in business strategy. No one could have asked for better account management colleagues than Margot Marshall, Jean Alexander, and Mary Stibal.

At Foote Cone & Belding I had the pleasure of working with John Loden, who remains a good friend. Also while at FCB I enjoyed working with Jack Boland, Jane Gardner, Liz Levy, and many other terrific account people.

At Ammirati Puris Lintas (now Lowe Lintas & Partners), I was fortunate to work with an impressive crew of account people, among them Nancy McNally, Lance Smith, Jeff Wilks, Rob Quish, Tom Sebok, Peter Fekula, Peter Leinroth, and Steve McCall.

Also at Ammirati, Cheryl Bailey and Sue Manber were terrific strategists to learn from, as was the incredibly smart Steve Gardner. Vivian Young is a deeply intuitive strategist, and one of the nicest people I ever have worked with. Mike Lotito and Ellen Wasserman taught me about media; Brian Cauley about the World Wide Web. Alyson Henning is the best new-business executive I've ever worked with.

No one is better at the business of the agency business than Ammirati's Phil Palazzo, who was the rock of that agency. I've been fortunate to have his support, encouragement, and friendship.

When Ammirati & Puris was still independent, Martin Puris pushed me to build something, to be an entrepreneur for the agency. Six years later, when I went out on my own, Martin became one of my first clients. I am very grateful for that push, and for that support. I also am grateful to Martin for asking me to be a part of the superb agency he and his partner Ralph Ammirati created.

Over the years I've had many terrific creative colleagues. At Bronner Slosberg: Rich Person, Tony Platt, Nancy Harhut, Phil Feemster, and Mitch Lunsford. At FCB: Hélène Côté and Fred Schwartz. At Ammirati: Tony Gomes, Tom Nelson, Doug Robinson, David Page, Brent Bouchez, David Wecal, Peter Rauch, Shelley Lanman, Carole Weitz, Tomas Mendez, Megan Skelly, and Michael O'Neal.

I learned much from Christine Bastoni, my creative partner at Bronner Slosberg and then later at FCB. She is a creative director of unusual talent and presence.

Many account people who worked for me were teachers as well as students. At Bronner Slosberg, there was Lisa Phildius Pierce, Andy Pierce, Ann Morgan, and Sheila Medico. From my FCB days I remember Heidi Oestrike, Sara Lucier, and Kevin Burke. At Ammirati, Debbie Elkins, Elizabeth Ebbert, Sandy Markham, Alison Fontaine Engel, Adrienne Wax, Lisa Lefebvre, Lori Goldfeder, Eddie Safdieh, Ann Woodward, and many others did terrific work during my tenure there.

I worked with my friend Liz Deutch for more than five years at Ammirati, and learned something from her every day.

Great clients are all too rare, but I've been fortunate to work with many. At American Express, it was always invigorating to work with Ann Busquet, Cyndi Grenafege, Bill Nutting, Lou Taffer, Ken Chenault, Mary Miller, Maria Miller, Abby Kohnstam, and Sally Ann Colonna. The House of Seagram's Richard Shaw is a thoughtful and forward-thinking client.

At Compaq I had the good fortune to work with Lynn Schlemeyer, Karen Jones, and Kelly Steffen Happ, superb clients all. Among his many other client virtues, Compaq's David Vining was especially effective in pushing for and supporting great work.

For nearly a decade I've relied on the friendship and advice of Don Wright. Don provided many helpful suggestions for this book.

I am especially indebted to Mike Slosberg, who wrote the introduction to this book. Mike is a wonderful friend, mentor, and former creative partner. I owe him more debts of thanks than I can possibly repay, but he, ever gracious, never calls in the chits.

I want to thank Richard Cline for supplying the book with his wonderfully droll perspective on the ad business. His drawings provide pleasurable relief to my various prescriptions, reminders, and points-of-view on account service. I also want to thank my many colleagues for contributing their succinct and insightful opinions on account service.

I am grateful to Jonathan Lippincott for his elegant and disciplined book design. My editors, Jana Eisenberg and Heidi Jacobs, saved me from the embarrassment of poor sentence construction and awkward syntax. If you discover any such errors in the book, rest assured they are entirely my fault, not my editors'.

Conversations with my father-in-law Bob Wilvers, a legendary creative director at Tinker and at Wells Rich Greene, among other agencies, confirmed the need for this book. If Bob were alive today, he and I would be arguing still about the value of account service.

My earliest lessons in account service came from my father, Abraham Martin. My dad never thought of himself as an account guy, but no one worked harder at forging relationships with clients than he.

Lastly, I could not have written this book without the loving support of my wife and partner Roberta, who is the best person I know at relationship building, and the best person I know, period.

RS
January 22, 2000

56 THINGS EVERY
ACCOUNT PERSON
SHOULD KNOW

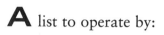 list to operate by:

20 PRESCRIPTIONS FOR GREAT ACCOUNT WORK

1. Great work wins business; a great relationship keeps it.
2. Live the client's brand.
3. Take on the coloration of your clients; do not compromise your character.
4. No matter how social it becomes, never forget it is business.
5. You cannot lead an account from your desk.
6. There is no such thing as too much communication.
7. Make no commitment without consultation.
8. There is no "no" in your client vocabulary.
9. Before you tell clients or colleagues what you *think*, tell them what you *know*.

10. Before you give clients what they *need*, make sure you give them what they *want*.

11. Fight *about* the work with colleagues, fight *for* it with clients.

12. Always think endgame.

13. No surprises about money or time.

14. Deal with trouble head-on.

15. Be brief, be bright, be gone.

16. Better to have it and not need it, than need it and not have it.

17. Once a client, always a client.

18. Forget what Stanley Motss said: "I want the credit."

19. If things go wrong, take the blame.

20. Judgement overrides any rule.

4 STEPS TO TAKE AT THE START OF ANY ASSIGNMENT

21. Always manage client expectations from the outset.

22. Define success.

23. Start with an agreed-on strategy, budget, and schedule.

24. Ask yourself, "What do my colleagues need to create great advertising?" Then deliver it.

5 PROCEDURES FOR A STRATEGY BRIEF

25. Provide the client's perspective.

26. Involve the creative team.

27. Get the client's input and approval.

28. Take the word "brief" seriously.

29. Know when to look it up; know when to make it up.

7 REMINDERS ABOUT MAKING GREAT CREATIVE

30. Always ask yourself, "Does this advertising pass the 'so-what' test?"

31. Don't fall in love with good work.

32. Don't fall for bad work.

33. Choice is good.

34. Do not "sell."

35. Bring your clients into the process early.

36. Respect what it takes to do great creative.

8 THOUGHTS ON CLIENT PRESENTATIONS

37. Client presentations are as important as new business presentations.

38. No understudies on presentation day.

39. No scenery chewers; no dead bodies.

40. Be prepared to throw away the script.

41. The more informal you want be, the more rehearsed you need to be.

42. Know your opening cold.

43. Support what you say.

44. Listening is more important than talking.

4 ELEMENTS OF BETTER MEETING MANAGEMENT

45. Start on time, end on time.

46. Have an agenda, stick to it.

47. Lead the meeting, don't dominate it.

48. Always follow up.

2 BOOKS TO READ AND REREAD

49. *The Elements of Style.*

50. *On Writing Well.*

1 SUGGESTION ON BEING A CONCIERGE TO YOUR CLIENTS

51. Be one.

4 POINTS OF VIEW ON PERSONAL STYLE

52. Make an investment in yourself.

53. Buy fewer, better pieces of tailored clothing.

54. Ask for style help if you need it.

55. Think uniform.

1 MORE THING TO REMEMBER

56. Remember to say thank you.

A NOTE ON THE TEXT

The text of this book is set in Sabon; the display face in Zurich. The paper is 60 lb. Finch Fine, bright white. Printing and binding by R. R. Donnelly & Sons Company. Designed by Jonathan D. Lippincott.